The Rose that
grew From
Concrete

The Rose That grew From Concrete

Tupac Amaru Shakur

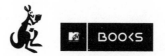

MTV BOOKS

POCKET BOOKS

NEW YORK LONDON TORONTO SYDNEY

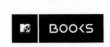 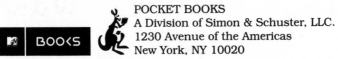

POCKET BOOKS
A Division of Simon & Schuster, LLC.
1230 Avenue of the Americas
New York, NY 10020

ISBN-13: 978-0-671-02845-9
ISBN-10:   0-671-02845-6

To Our Children

We must support our children in every way we can. We must allow our children freedom to express themselves creatively. We must praise our children and thank them for their gift of inspiration. We must motivate our children spiritually. We must challenge our children to a higher level of achievement. We must increase our children's self-confidence and improve their overall quality of life.

So we say to our children, draw, paint, write, act, sing, dance, think, express, and be free to dream always: Nzingha, Malik, Imani, Zahra, Keon, Lil Jamala, Mia, Kyira, Avani, Maya, Jasmine B., Ineke, Maja, Jacia, Jemil, Yusef, Rubiyah, Helen, Jada, Carl, Milan, Seleick, Ashaki, Valencia, Adaija, Lianna, Lil Imani, Alai, Kai, Alana, Remi, Rylie, Etan, Leigh, Shaquan, Talia, Devanee, Nikko, Demouria, Alana, Henry III, Marquessa, Emily, Audrey, Andrew, Alyssa, Mathew, Brooke, Alex, Arielle, Jonothan, Ashley, Kayla, Jax, Rafi, Chan'tal, and Coy.

Contents

THE ROSE THAT GREW FROM CONCRETE

NOTHING CAN COME BETWEEN US

JUST A BREATH OF FREEDOM

LIBERTY NEEDS GLASSES

Acknowledgments

Tupac, I am grateful to God for the most precious gift of your life, your friendship, your love, and your indomitably honest, true spirit! Sekyiwa, Wonderful Woman! Sweet Child! Courageous Mother and Sister! Thank you for walking this earth with me! Nzingha and Malik, we continue to try to be better at preparing you for this world and this world for you! Create, love, and laugh! Gloria Jean and family, my sister who has been our rock for over fifty years—we are the only children of Rosa Belle and Walter Williams Jr. I know they are smiling because we remember our duty to family. Outlawz. Our Baltimore family. Our Lumberton family. Lisa Lee, My Team/Rick Fischbein, Donald David, Beth Fischbein, Jeff Glassman, Linda Amaya, Sandy Fox, Dina LaPolt, and crew. Jeff Joiner and family. Rick Barlowe and family. Henry Faison and family. Devanee, Talia, and Nikko. The entire Johnson family, especially Sandra for the food and the original eggroll recipe that fed Tupac for years. Belvie Rooks, Ebony Jo-Ann, Sonia Sanchez, Nikki Giovanni, Kathleen, Ignae, Angela, Lyle, and Elanor Gittens, Jasmine, Karolyn, Gigi, Charlene, Charis Henry, Akilah, Cynthia McKinney, and Tre'mayne Maxie, Dana, Tom Whalley, Liza Joseph, The Shakur Family Foundation, Thomas McCreary, Carl, Staci, Felicia, and all of our friends who have picked our spirits up during this journey into the light. We love you all! Joey Arbagey (KMEL). Tracy Sherrod, Eduardo Braniff, Calaya Reid, Jack Horner,

Mike Mitchell, and Toby, Emily Bestler, Kara Welsh, Liate Stehlik, Anthony Goff, Paolo Pepe, Jeanne Lee, Liz Brooks, Lisa Silfen, John De Laney, Stephen Fallert, thank you, thank you. Molly, for being the connector, the juggler, the struggler. You are stuck having to pull all the pieces together. Thank you for all the writing, reading, rereading, and for your effective communication skills. We all need you! Do we tell you enough? Jamal Joseph, Arvand Elihu, and James Cavinal. Poetry Circle/Lawanda Hunter, Ray Luv (Raymond Tyson) Damond, Jacinta, T. J., Lotoya Gilel, Uilani Enid, Arrow, and Monica Mcknight. Dimpho and Tebojo. Young Imaginations, AIM, Kidz Voices, Kaleidoscope, International Women's Convention, and Ashkenaz in Berkeley. All the high schools that let us read our poetry before the rest of the world gave us their permission. Corina Abouaf. Reese Hogg, David and Herb Steinberg. Mac Mall. Tracy Robinson and Gobi. Talia and Devanee.

—AFENI SHAKUR

• • •

My children, Shaquan, Talia, Devanee, Naikko, and all my other children, you are the reason I do this, my cup runnith over. Afeni Shakur, you gave your only son to not just me, but to the world. So many times when I have not had the strength to even get out of bed, it is Pac's spirit that gives me breath. It is you who gave his spirit breath, for this and for allowing me to continue his work, I cannot put into words my gratitude. Thank you. Tupac, I will continue to do your work with the portion of my soul that you didn't take with you.

—LEILA STEINBERG

Preface

Celebrate life
through the music
through the spoken word
through the splatter of
    color on paper
    or wood
    or iron
    or canvas
But celebrate your life
Celebrate your ability
    to feel joy and
    sadness
Celebrate your ability to feel!
Only then will we be free to
Feel!

I thank God and all my ancestors for the Artistic Tupac, for the Poetic Tupac. There was never a day when Tupac did not appreciate language. The sound and the rhythm of words did not intimidate him. He sought to interpret his world using all the visual and linguistic tools available to him. The battle between the discipline of intellect and the ravings of the soul is a fascinating one.

These poems were written from 1989 to 1991, reflecting the heart and soul of my son. They represent the process of a young artist's journey to understand and accept a world of unthinkable contradictions. I always believed Tupac's work can and does speak for itself. I have nothing to add or detract—my responsibility is to do all I can to make sure he has been heard in venues and milieus that are appropriate to what he himself gave to his life and his work.

Tupac put these poems in the safekeeping of Leila Steinberg, who was Tupac's first professional manager and adult friend. We are indebted to Leila for her integrity in looking after the safety of Tupac's work. Her loyalty has allowed us the ability to offer this work in this medium.

Tupac had quite a few friends whose actions regarding his artistic integrity reflect a subconscious belief that he is still in the room. We thank all those of his peers, friends, and business associates who continue to act as though Tupac were still in the room. Thank you my beautiful and wonderful son—you're a perfect mirror of my soul!

> When you're not here
> I measure the space
> You used to occupy.
> Large areas become
> vast and endless
> deserts of you
> not there.

—AFENI SHAKUR

Foreword: Tupac, C U in Heaven

I'm glad this collection of the poetry of Tupac Shakur is being published. Those of us who recognize not only genius but light knew early on that young Shakur was special. He lit up the screen in *Juice* and *Above the Rim.* His raps were tight and strong. We all said to ourselves, "Something good is coming."

I guess it will always be the case that when someone brings a new idea or, more accurately, a truthful idea there will be complaints. There will always be those people, especially those people who are wrong, who try to shut the truth and daring down. I remember when *The Sugar Hill Gang* started the "New Rap Revolution" and they were fun. Grandmothers in stupid movies could imitate their rap, and old men could return from *Cocoon* and break-dance. It was just so, well, cute to play off rap. Then along came Tupac. You don't see any senior take-offs on his art. You don't see Hume Cronyn and his friends hip-hopping down the street to *Holler If Ya Hear Me*. No garden parties with Grandma bopping up to *Something 2 Die 4*. So they found a name, Gangsta Rap, to somehow distinguish it from, what? Polite, nice, highly compromised rap? They tried to isolate that beautiful boy who was trying to bring on the truth so that they could flood us with lies and excuses.

People will still stand up and say really stupid things like "I don't think profane language should be used" or "They are always cursing and stuff, and I think they can make their point without bad language." But I always think bad language is "school vouchers," "lower taxes on capital gains," "don't ask don't tell," and language like that, which, silently or not so silently, kills people who are different from what we want to think we are. But who, in truth, are not so different after all. Children have to be educated; the correct citizens to pay taxes are those who have money; people have a right to their own hearts, but mostly what I keep seeing is the emptiness of lives that have nothing better to do than judge and condemn. Tupac once said, "Only God can judge me." I say good for him. He had taken that step to understand that no matter what any of them say you have an obligation to the universe to follow your own muse.

I like Tupac Shakur in the same way I liked Prince when he was Prince. When he wrote music that was a bit edgy, a bit out there, a bit daring. Whatever turned that beautiful boy, the "rude boy," into a whiny symbol should rot in five different hells. Tupac stayed fresh and strong and committed to himself and his people. Yet, as this collection shows, he was a sensitive soul. The poems for the lovers in this life, for his mother, for his child in heaven show a boy who touches our souls. This, too, is Tupac. Just as people want to make Malcolm X an integrationist, thereby changing the nature of his daring and his truth, people want us to overlook the sensitivity and love Tupac Shakur shows because, after all, if he loves, if he cries, if he cares, if he, in other words, is not a monster, then what have we done? What a great crime has been committed in the name of, what, the status quo? How awful and ugly of us.

One day, in the not too distant future, there will be a gathering in Atlanta much like the one in Memphis. You remember

Memphis and Graceland. The Postmaster General of the United States invited Elvis's family members to unveil the artists' concepts of Elvis. There was an 800 number for the young, pretty, slim Elvis and another 800 number for the fat, drugged-out Elvis. We the public were invited to phone in our choice, and that would be the stamp. When the Malcolm X stamp was chosen, there was no gathering at Betty Shabazz's home. No calling the girls, Malcolm and Betty's daughters, together with the Postmaster General. No artists' conception, inviting the public to choose between a smiling Malcolm and that frowny ugly thing they produced. No choice between a Malcolm-and-Betty stamp and a Malcolm-by-himself stamp. In fact, as usual, white people decided what Black people should want and did as they wished with the image of our hero. The Tupac Stamp must go public. We, the public, demand the right to make choices. I want an image of a thoughtful Tupac with the words: *C U in Heaven*. He deserves to be taken seriously and we must therefore mourn.

—Nikki Giovanni

Introduction

Tupac felt that through art we could incite a new revolution that incorporated the heart, mind, body, spirit, and soul. He wanted his art to instill honesty, integrity, and respect.

It was the spring of 1989 in Marin City, when a young man with fan-like eyelashes, overflowing charisma, and the most infectious laugh began to make his way into my life. I was sitting on the grass outside Bayside Elementary School reading Winnie Mandela's *Part of My Soul Went with Him*. A young man with big beautiful sparkling eyes came up behind me quoting lines aloud from the book. It fascinated me that he knew the lines by heart. When he introduced himself as Tupac, I realized that he was the Tupac that friends had spoken to me about. I was a writer and producer working in the music industry and he was an aspiring rapper looking for a manager. I did not have time to speak at length with him then because I had a class to teach, a multicultural educational program, "Young Imaginations." However, I was so impressed with him that I invited him to sit in on my class.

After class, Tupac began to share his ideas on how the arts could be included in school curriculums to help youth address some of the issues that they were experiencing in their lives. By combining art with education, Tupac felt we could begin to heal society's pain and confusion.

I later invited him to participate in a weekly writing circle I had at my house. His first time there, he immediately took over and decided that we would write about what he wanted, not what I wanted. One of the first poems Tupac wrote with us—"The Rose That Grew from Concrete"—tells you a great deal about him in just a few lines. Tupac was the rose that grew in spite of all obstacles. His life shows that a young man/boy could rise, shine, grow, and bloom beyond overbearing conditions to become one of America's most beloved men. He also had the grace to make it all look easy. Tupac's accomplishments, in twenty-five years, far surpass what most people do in three of his lifetimes. These poetry circles continued for a long time. We were all broke and struggling, but Tupac was the only one who had ever really tasted poverty; only he could take potatoes when there was no meat and make the best tacos you ever tasted; and only he could make a gourmet meal out of Top-Ramen noodles. He was a genius who became the group's greatest inspiration. Within four weeks of our meeting, Tupac appointed me his manager.

It has been several years since Tupac has passed, and a day does not go by that I do not think of him. I have kept a collection of the many poems that he wrote during the time of our poetry circle. The following poems show a side of Tupac Amaru Shakur that popular culture has yet to realize existed—pensive, introspective, loving, and concerned about world affairs. There is no better way to get inside the mind and heart of an artist than to examine his artistic expressions. I hope these poems allow those who are fascinated by Tupac to see his sensitivity, insight, revolutionary mind, fears, passion, and sense of humor. Tupac's stature and recognition as a rapper is clear and unequivocal. However, his place as a literary artist/poet has yet to be recognized.

I hope these poems, which Tupac wrote from his heart, will encourage people to take the first steps necessary to see his literary importance, as well as have us acknowledge the life struggles of young black men. Written when Tupac was nineteen, this poetry is free from the restraints of the music industry and all monetary pressures. It is free of the anger that came from getting shot, betrayed, and thrown in jail for a crime I believe he never committed. It is Tupac before his fame.

For the past seven years, Tupac's writings have been one of my most powerful teaching tools. I have participated in programs in schools, youth facilities, and a number of prisons all over the country. My most exciting work began in 1997 when Arvand Elihu invited me to participate in *History 98: The Poetry and History of Tupac Shakur.* This was a class Arvand was developing at UC Berkeley. Students from all races and backgrounds participated, discussing such issues as single parenting and poverty. Students and universities throughout the country have requested the teaching materials that Arvand compiled to initiate their own Tupac curriculum. Tupac was finally being recognized by academia.

In the summer of 1998, I assisted Afeni Shakur, Tupac's mother, in developing the first annual summer youth conference, "Life Goes On." We spent more than a weekend in Sparta, Georgia, using Tupac's lyrics to conduct workshops that resulted in bringing new life into the hearts and minds of those in attendance. Participants traveled from all over the nation to take advantage of the healing tool Tupac left us, his words. The following August, I was invited as a delegate to the International Women's Convention in Johannesburg, South Africa, to conduct a workshop with Enid Picket on the power of art in education. Once again the curriculum was based around

Tupac's writings. I have since been invited to the Netherlands and Costa Rica to conduct similar programming.

Now, Tupac's work, and especially these poems, are available to the public. I hope that they can attract the attention of those who have not given Tupac a fair chance—the same people who are quick to judge Tupac based on the media's sometimes negative portrayal. Tupac's poems can teach us about universal needs that textbooks rarely address. Poems such as "And 2morrow" and "Still I Wait for Dawn" speak of the need to survive and wait for a better day. They also teach us that humanity as a whole suffers if anyone starves. Unfortunately, it took his death to teach us that when one man dies we all bleed.

—LEILA STEINBERG

The Rose That grew From Concrete

The Rose That Grew From Concrete

AutoBiographical

Did u Hear about THe rose that grew from a cracK
in the concrete
Proving Nature's Laws wrong it learned 2 walk
without Having FeeT
Funny it seems But By Keeping its Dreams
it learned 2 BreaTHe fresh air
Long Live THe rose That grew from Concrete
when no one else even cared!

The Rose That Grew from Concrete
Autobiographical

Did u hear about the rose that grew from a crack
in the concrete
Proving nature's laws wrong it learned 2 walk
without having feet
Funny it seems but by keeping its dreams
it learned 2 breathe fresh air
Long live the rose that grew from concrete
when no one else even cared!

In The Depths Of Solitude

Dedicated 2 me

I exist in the depths of Solitude
pondering my true goal
Trying 2 find peace of mind
and still preserve my soul
Constantly yearning 2 be accepted
and from all receive respect
Never compromising but sometimes Risky
and that is my only Regret
A young ♥ with an old Soul
How can there be ☮
How can 👁 be in the depths of Solitude
when there R 2 inside of me
This Duo within me causes
the perfect opportunity
2 learn and live twice as fast
as those who accept simplicity

In the Depths of Solitude

Dedicated 2 Me

I exist in the depths of solitude
pondering my true goal
Trying 2 find peace of mind
and still preserve my soul
CONSTANTLY yearning 2 be accepted
and from all receive respect
Never compromising but sometimes risky
and that is my only regret
A young heart with an old soul
how can there be peace
How can I be in the depths of solitude
when there R 2 inside of me
This Duo within me causes
the perfect opportunity
2 learn and live twice as fast
as those who accept simplicity

Some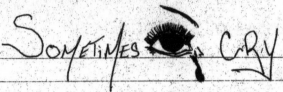times Cry

Sometimes when I'm alone
I cry because I'm on my own
The tears I cry R Bitter and warm
They flow with life but take no form
I cry Because my Heart is Torn
and I find it difficult 2 carry on
if I had an ear 2 confide in
I would cry among my treasured friends
But who Do u know that stops that long
To help another carry on
The world moves fast and it would rather pass u by
than 2 stop and c what makes u cry
It's painful and Sad and Sometimes I cry
and no one cares about why.

Sometimes I Cry

Sometimes when I'm alone
I cry because I'm on my own
The tears I cry R bitter and warm
They flow with life but take no form
I cry because my heart is torn
and I find it difficult 2 carry on
If I had an ear 2 confide in
I would cry among my treasured friends
But who do u know that stops that long
to help another carry on
The world moves fast and it would rather pass u by
than 2 stop and c what makes u cry
It's painful and sad and sometimes I cry
and no one cares about why.

Under The Skies Above

After the Miscarriage

my child is out there somewhere
under the skies above
waiting anxiously 4 u and me
2 bless it with our love
a part of me a part of u
and a part of this love we share
will protect my unborn child
Who lives dormant out there somewhere
Sometimes in my dreams
I imagine what it would be like
How could I properly guide him
when even I don't know what's right
whether he is born in wealth or poverty
There will be no deficiency in love
I welcome this gift of life
given from GOD under the skies above

Under the Skies Above

After the Miscarriage

My child is out there somewhere
under the skies above
waiting anxiously 4 u and me
2 bless it with our love
A part of me a part of u
and a part of this love we share
will protect my unborn child
who lives dormant out there somewhere
Sometimes in my dreams
I imagine what it would be like
How could I properly guide him
when even I don't know what's right
Whether he is born in wealth or poverty
there will be no deficiency in love
I welcome this gift of life
given from GOD under the skies above

LIFE THROUGH MY eyes

Life through my Bloodshot eyes
would scare a square 2 death
Poverty, murder, violence
and never a moment 2 rest
fun and games R few
But treasured like gold 2 me
cuz I realize that I must return
2 my spot in Poverty
But mock my words when I say
my heart will not exist
unless my destiny comes through
and puts and end 2 all of this

Life Through My Eyes

Life through my bloodshot eyes
would scare a square 2 death
poverty, murder, violence
and never a moment 2 rest
Fun and games R few
but treasured like gold 2 me
cuz I realize that I must return
2 my spot in poverty
But mock my words when I say
my heart will not exist
unless my destiny comes through
and puts an end 2 all of this

WHEN Ure Heart TURNS CoLD
          2 KRISTEN & my other Friends
              WHO WoNDeR

WHEN your HearT TurNS cold
iT causes your Soul 2 Freeze
~~instead of~~
IT spreads Throughout your spirit
like a ruthless feeling disease
The walls that once were Down
Now stand firm and tall
Safe From Hate/Love, pain/Joy
until u feel Nothing at all
When ure heart TurNs cold
   a Baby's cry means Nothing
   A Dead corpse is trivial
   Mothers neglecteds children is Daily
   Lonliness Becomes your routine friend
   Death seems like Tranquility
   Sleeping is Never pleasant
      if u even sleep at all
   u forget ideals and Turn off the reason,
   2 make Sure the product gets sold
   You Dont understand How I Behave
   Just wait til your heart Turns cold!

When Ure Heart Turns Cold

2 Kristen & My Other Friends
Who Wonder

When your heart turns cold
it causes your soul 2 freeze
It spreads throughout your spirit
like a ruthless feeling disease
The walls that once were down
now stand firm and tall
Safe from hate/love, pain/joy
until u feel nothing at all
When ure heart turns cold
a baby's cry means nothing
A dead corpse is trivial
Mothers neglecting children is daily
Loneliness becomes your routine friend
Death seems like tranquility
Sleeping is never pleasant
if u even sleep at all
u forget ideals and turn off the reason
2 make sure the product gets sold
You don't understand how I behave
Just wait till your heart turns Cold!

UNTITLED

Please wake me when I'm free
I cannot bear captivity
where my culture I'm told holds no significance
I'll wither and die in ignorance
But my inner eye can c a race
who reigned as Kings in another place
The green of trees were Rich and full
and every man spoke of Beautiful —
men and women together as equals
War was gone because all was peaceful
But now like a nightmare I wake 2 c
that I live like a prisoner of Poverty
Please wake me when I'm free
I cannot bear captivity
4) I would rather be stricken blind
~~If I co~~ Than 2 live without expression of mind

Untitled

Please wake me when I'm free
I cannot bear captivity
where my culture I'm told holds no significance
I'll wither and die in ignorance
But my inner eye can c a race
who reigned as kings in another place
the green of trees were rich and full
and every man spoke of beautiful
men and women together as equals
War was gone because all was peaceful
But now like a nightmare I wake 2 c
That I live like a prisoner of poverty
Please wake me when I'm free
I cannot bear captivity
4 I would rather be stricken blind
than 2 live without expression of mind

THE ETERNAL LAMENT

FROM my mind 2 the Depths of my Soul
I yearn 2 achieve all of my goals
And all of my Free Time will Be Spent
On the 1's I miss I will Lament

I am Not a Perfectionist
But still I seek Perfection
I am Not a great Romantic
But yet I yearn 4 affection

ETERNally My mind will Produce
Ways 2 put My talents 2 use
and when I'm done No matter where I've been
I'll yearn 2 Do it all again.

The Eternal Lament

From my mind 2 the depths of my soul
I yearn 2 achieve all of my goals
And all of my free time will be spent
On the 1's I miss I will lament

I am not a perfectionist
But still I seek perfection
I am not a great romantic
But yet I yearn 4 affection

Eternally my mind will produce
ways 2 put my talents 2 use
and when I'm done no matter where I've been
I'll yearn 2 do it all again.

Only 4 the Righteous

I'm Down with Strictly Dope "So"
That means I'm More than u handle
"Hot" I'm hotter than the wax from
  a candle
"Him" That's Roc he's my microphone Companion
"Lyrics" Full of Knowledge Truth and understanding
"Hobbies" Rapping is my only recreation
"Retire" u must Be on some kind of Medication
"Why" because I'll never loosen up my mic grip
"Drugs" never cuz I'm living on the right tip
"Sex" only with my girl because I love her
"Babies" impossible I always use a Rubber
"Bored" rarely cuz I'm keeping myself Busy
"Scratch" nah I leave the cutting up 2 Dize
"Dize?" yeh That's my D.J. he's the greatest
"WORD" noh he's paying me 2 Say this
"the MIND" is something that I cultivate
  and Treasure
"Thanks" your welcome and besides it was
  my Pleasure

Only 4 the Righteous

I'm Down with strictly Dope "So"
That means I'm more than u can handle
"Hot" I'm hotter than the wax from
　　a candle
"Him" that's Roc he's my microphone companion
"Lyrics" full of knowledge truth and understanding
"Hobbies" rapping is my only recreation
"retire" u must be on some kind of medication
"why" because I'll never loosen up my mic grip
"Drugs" never cuz I'm living on the right tip
"sex" only with my girl because I love her
"Babies" impossible I always use a rubber
"Bored" rarely cuz I'm keeping myself busy
"Scratch" nah I leave the cutting up 2 Dize
"Dize?" yeh that's my D.J. he's the greatest
"Word" nah he's paying me 2 say this
"the mind" is something that I cultivate
　　and treasure
"Thanks" you're welcome and besides it was
　　my Pleasure

WHAT OF FAME ?

everyone knows ure FACE
THe world Screams ure NAME
Never again R u ALONe

What of Fame?

everyone knows ure Face
The world screams ure name
Never again R u alone

-(THE SHINING STAR Within)

DEDICATED 2 Marilyn Monroe

Seceets R hidden within the clouds
OF Darkness,
And in this place No one Dares 2 Breathe
In Fear of self expression
It has been This way
forever AND a Day
until She came 2 Shine
with a Spark of innocence and questions
ONLy 2 be answered with Darkness
NoT just Darkness but the Silent Kind
that steals your Soul and Kills your mind
There was No Compassion
for this thriving star
only exploitations
and confused Jealousy
u Saw no hope and brought the end
Never aknowledging the star within

The Shining Star Within!
Dedicated 2 Marilyn Monroe

Secrets R hidden within the clouds
of Darkness,
And in this place no one Dares 2 Breathe
in Fear of self-expression
It has been this way
forever and a day
until she came 2 shine
with a spark of innocence and questions
only 2 be answered with Darkness
Not just Darkness but the silent kind
that steals your soul and kills your mind
There was no compassion
for this thriving star
only exploitations
and confused jealousy
u saw no hope and brought the end
Never acknowledging the star within

STARRY NIGHT

Dedicated in memory of
Vincent Van Gogh

a creative heart, obsessed with satisfying
this dormant and uncaring society
u have given them the stars at night
and u have given them Bountiful Bouquets of Sunflowers
But 4 u there is only contempt
and though u pour yourself into that frame
and present it so proudly
this world could not accept your Masterpieces
from the heart

So on that starry night
U gave 2 us and
U took away from us
The one thing we never acknowledged
your Life

Starry Night

Dedicated in Memory of
Vincent van Gogh

a creative heart, obsessed with satisfying

This dormant and uncaring society

u have given them the stars at night

and u have given them Bountiful Bouquets of Sunflowers

But 4 u there is only contempt

and though u pour yourself into that frame

and present it so proudly

this world could not accept your masterpieces

from the heart

So on that starry night

u gave 2 us and

u took away from us

The one thing we never acknowledged

   your life

IF I FAIL

If in my quest 2 achieve my goals
I stumble or crumble and lose my soul
Those that knew me would easily co-sign
There was never a life as hard as mine
No father — No money — No chance and NO guide
I only follow my voice inside
if it guides me wrong and I do not win
I'll learn from mistakes and try 2 achieve again

If I Fail

If in my quest 2 achieve my goals
I stumble or crumble and lose my soul
Those that knew me would easily co-sign
There was never a life as hard as mine
No father—no money—no chance and no guide
I only follow my voice inside
if it guides me wrong and I do not win
I'll learn from mistakes and try 2 achieve again.

WHAT IS IT THAT 👁 SEARCH 4

I KNOW NOT WHAT I SEARCH 4
BUT I KNOW I HAVE YET 2 FIND IT,
BECAUSE IT IS INVISIBLE 2 THE 👁
MY HEART MUST SEARCH 4 IT BLINDED.

AND IF BY CHANCE I FIND IT,
WILL I KNOW MY MISSION IS ACHIEVED?
CAN ONE COME 2 CONCLUSIONS,
BEFORE THE QUESTION IS CONCEIVED?

JUST AS NO ONE KNOWS
WHAT LIES BEYOND THE SHORE,
I WILL NEVER FIND THE ANSWER 2
WHAT IT IS THAT I SEARCH 4.

What Is It That I Search 4

I know not what I search 4
But I know I have yet 2 find it,
Because it is invisible 2 the eye
My heart must search 4 it blinded.

And if by chance I find it,
Will I know my mission is achieved?
Can one come 2 conclusions,
Before the question is conceived?

Just as no one knows
what lies beyond the shore,
I will never find the answer 2
what it is that I search 4.

The Fear in the Heart of a Man
Dedicated 2 my heart

against an attacker I will Boldly Take My stand
Because My heart will show Fear 4 No Man
But 4 a Broken heart I run with fright
scared 2 Be Blind in a vulnerable night
I Believe This Fear is in every man
Some will aknowledge it others will feil 2 understand
There is No fear in a shallow heart
Because shallow hearts Don't fall apart
But feeling hearts that truly care
are fragile 2 the flow of air
and if I am 2 Be true then I must give
My fragile heart
I May receive great Joy or u May return it
ripped apart

The Fear in the Heart of a Man
Dedicated 2 My Heart

against an attacker I will boldly take my stand
because my heart will show fear 4 no man
but 4 a broken heart I run with fright
scared 2 be blind in a vulnerable night
I believe this fear is in every man
some will acknowledge it others will fail 2 understand
there is no fear in a shallow heart
because shallow hearts don't fall apart
but feeling hearts that truly care
are fragile 2 the flow of air
and if I am 2 be true then I must give
my fragile heart
I may receive great joy or u may return it
ripped apart

GOD

WHEN I was Alone AND had Nothing
I asked 4 a friend 2 help me bear the
pain No one came except... GOD

when I needed a breath 2 rise
from my sleep No one could
help me except .... GOD

When All I saw was Sadness
and I needed Answers no one
heard me except .... GOD

So when I am asked who I
give my unconditional love 2
Look For No other Name
except ..... GOD!

God

when I was alone and had nothing
I asked 4 a friend 2 help me bear the
pain no one came except . . . GOD

when I needed a breath 2 rise
from my sleep no one could
help me except . . . . GOD

when all I saw was sadness
and I needed answers no one
heard me except . . . . GOD

so when I am asked who I
give my unconditional love 2
look for no other name
except . . . . . GOD!

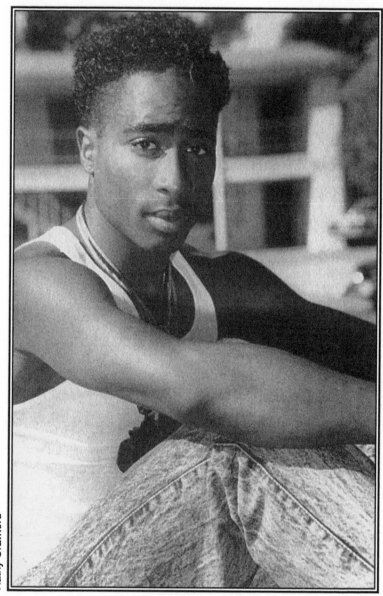

NOTHING CAN
Come Between us

NOTHING Can Come Between us
4 JOHN

let's Not talk of Money
let us forget The WORLD
4 a moment let's Just revel
iN our eternal comradery
iN my Heart I kNow
there will Never Be a DAy
That I DoN't remember
the times we shared
u were a friend
when I was at my lowest
and being a friend 2 me
was Not easy Nor feshionable
Regardless of how popular
I become u remain
my unconditional friend
unconditional iN its truest Sense
Did u think I would forget
Did u 4 one moment Dream
that I would ignore u
if so Remember this from here 2 forever
Nothing Can Come between us

Nothing Can Come Between Us

4 John

let's not talk of money
let us forget the world
4 a moment let's just revel
in our eternal comradery
in my Heart I know
there will never be a day
that I don't remember
the times we shared
u were a friend
when I was at my lowest
and being a friend 2 me
was not easy or fashionable
regardless of how popular
I become u remain
my unconditional friend
unconditional in its truest sense
did u think I would forget
did u 4 one moment dream
that I would ignore u
if so remember this from here 2 forever
nothing can come between us

My Dearest One!!

There R no words 2 express
How much 🖐, truly care
So Many Times 🖐, fantasize of
Feelings we can share
My ❤ has never known
The joy u bring 2 me
As if GOD knew what 🖐 wanted
and made u a reality
I'd die 2 hold u or 2 kiss u
or merely 2 c your face
My stomach quivers my body shivers
and my ❤ increases pace
2 give me $ or lots of gold
would not be the same 2 me
🖐, prayed and watched the distant stars
and finally u came 2 me!

Faithfully yours,

2pac

My Dearest One!!

There R no words 2 express
how much I truly care
So many times I fantasize of
feelings we can share
My heart has never known
the Joy u bring 2 me
As if GOD knew what I wanted
and made u a reality
I'd die 2 hold u or 2 kiss u
or merely to see your face
my stomach quivers my body shivers
and my heart increases pace
2 give me $ or lots of gold
would not be the same 2 me
I prayed and watched the distant stars
and finally u came 2 me!

If THERE BE PAIN...

If There Be Pain,
All u Need 2 DO
is call on me 2 Be with u
And Before u hang up the Phone
u will no longer be alone
Together we can never fall
Because our love will conquer all

If There Be Pain,
Reach out 4 a helping hand
and I shall hold u wherever I am
Every Breath I Breathe will be into u
4 without u here my Joy is through
my life was lived through falling rain
so call on me if there be pain

Faithfully
Yours,
Tupac
Amaru

19

If There Be Pain . . .

If there be pain,
  all u need 2 do
is call on me 2 be with u
And before u hang up the phone
u will no longer be alone
Together we can never fall
because our love will conquer all

If there be pain,
  reach out 4 a helping hand
and I shall hold u wherever I am
Every breath I breathe will be into u
4 without u here my joy is through
my life was lived through falling rain
so call on me if there be pain

THINGS THAT MAKE Hearts Break

pretty smiles
Deceiving laughs
and people who Dream with thier eyes open
Lonely children
Unanswered cries
and souls who have given up hoping
The other thing that breaks Hearts
R fairy tales that never come true
and selfish people who lie 2 me
selfish people Just like u

Things That Make Hearts Break

pretty smiles
deceiving laughs
and people who dream with their eyes open
lonely children
unanswered cries
and souls who have given up hoping
The other thing that breaks hearts
R fairy tales that never come true
and selfish people who lie 2 me
selfish people just like u

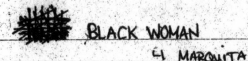

BLACK WOMAN
4 MARQUITA

THE DAY I MET u I saw strength
and I knew From that point on
that u were pure women 2 me
possessing a spirit that was strong

I want smiles 2 replace the sorrow
That u have encountered in the past
and since it was stre th that attracted me 2 u
it will take strength 2 make it last

my negative side will attempt 2 change u
But please Fight that with your all
it will be your strength that keep us Both Standing
while others around us Fall

Black Woman

The day I met u I saw strength
and I knew from that point on
that u were pure woman 2 me
possessing a spirit that was strong

I want smiles 2 replace the sorrow
that u have encountered in the past
and since it was strength that attracted me 2 u
it will take strength 2 make it last

My negative side will attempt 2 change u
but please fight that with your all
it will be your strength that keep us both standing
while others around us fall

And Still I Love u

I don't have everything
as a matter of fact I don't have anything
except a Dream of a Better Day
and you 2 help me find my way
Being a Man I am sure 2 make mistakes
But 2 keep u I would do all it takes
and if it meant my love was really True
I'd gladly die and watch over u
I wish u knew how much I cared
u'd see my love is True By the life we'd share
Even if u changed your mind and said our love was Thru
I'd want 2 die continuously cry and still I'd love u

And Still I Love U

I don't have everything
as a matter of fact I don't have anything
except a dream of a better day
and you 2 help me find my way
Being a man I am sure 2 make mistakes
but 2 keep u I would do all it takes
and if it meant my love was really true
I'd gladly die and watch over u
I wish u knew how much I cared
u'd see my love is true by the life we'd share
Even if u changed your mind and said our love was thru
I'd want 2 die continuously cry and still I'd love u

THE MUTUAL 'HEARTACHE?

INTRODUCED with innocence
who would have ever guessed
That u were the one I had
been so desperately searching 4
u talk as I do but yet u dont
understand when I mumble
u c as I do but your vision is
blurred by naivity
This is the barrier that separates us
I cannot cross yet
There is 2 much of me that
would frighten u so I live in
heartache because we cannot
fully explore this love and
what ot your heartache
Does it feel as sharp as mine
no matter where I go or how long it takes
I will never recover from this Mutual ♡ache.

The Mutual Heartache?

Introduced with innocence
who would have ever guessed
that u were the one I had
been so desperately searching 4
u talk as I do but yet u don't
understand when I mumble
u c as I do but your vision is
blurred by naivete
This is the barrier that separates us
I cannot cross yet
There is 2 much of me that
would frighten u so I live in
heartache because we cannot
fully explore this love and
what of your heartache
Does it feel as sharp as mine
No matter where I go or how long it takes
I will never recover from this mutual heartache.

1ST IMPRESSIONS
4 IRENE

Just when I thought I'd seen it all
our paths crossed and met
and I knew from the first glance
that u would be hard 2 4get
your eyes attracted me first
But you reeked of sultry confidence
I couldn't wait 2 touch lips
and kiss with my heart's intentions
when we did it was what I expected
and 4 that moment we erased the tension
of the awkwardness of first date jitters
and the initial blind date first impressions
we kissed again and I felt the passion
and this was CUPID'S blessing

1st Impressions

4 Irene

Just when I thought I'd seen it all
our paths crossed and met
and I knew from the First glance
that u would be hard 2 4get
your eyes attracted me First
but you reeked of sultry confidence
I couldn't wait 2 touch lips
and kiss with my Heart's intentions
when we did it was what I expected
and 4 that moment we erased the tension
of the awkwardness of First Date Jitters
and the initial Blind Date First impressions
we kissed again and I felt the passion
and this was CUPID's blessing

A Love Unspoken

WHAT OF A LOVE UNSPOKEN? is it weaker without a name
Does this Love deserve 2 exist without a title
Because I Dare NOT share its name
Does that make me cruel and cold
2 Deny the world of my salvation
Because I chose 2 let it grow
People TEND 2 choke
That which they Do NOT understand
Why Shouldn't I be weary
and withhold this love from MAN
what of a love unspoken
No one ever Knows
But this is a love that lasts
and in secrecy it grows

B

A Love Unspoken

What of a love unspoken? Is it weaker without a name?
Does this love deserve 2 exist without a title
because I dare not share its name
Does that make me cruel and cold
2 deny the world of my salvation
because I chose 2 let it grow
People tend 2 choke
that which they do not understand
Why shouldn't I be weary
and withhold this love from MAN
What of a love unspoken
no one ever knows
But this is a love that lasts
and in secrecy it grows

FOREVER AND TODAY

u say that u'll love me forever But what about today
As the Dusks Become Dawns and the years pass on will u love me the same
if so let us rejoice and Bathe in constant Pleasure
if not spare my heart today and I shall recover Before forever
And if my Doubts and ?'s upset u, forgive my fragile heart
I Just wanted 2 know if u'd love me forever
Before today would START!

Forever and Today

U say that u'll love me forever but what about today
As the dusks become dawns and the years pass on will u
    love me the same way
if so let us rejoice and bathe in constant pleasure
if not spare my heart today and I shall recover before
    forever
And if my doubts and ?'s upset u, forgive my fragile heart
I just wanted 2 know if you'd love me forever
before today would start!

WHEN I DO KISS u

I haven't yet for reasons of your own
But soon I'm sure you'll tire from being alone
u haven't recovered from the pain of the past
So u show me affection behind the wall of glass
But when I do finally kiss u
u will realize at last my heart was true

When I Do Kiss U

I haven't yet for reasons of your own
But soon I'm sure you'll tire from being alone
u haven't recovered from the pain of the past
So u show me affection behind the wall of glass
But when I do finally kiss u
u will realize at last my heart was true

Carmencita of the Bronx!

DEDICATED 2 Carmen

u SAW INNOCENCE at its BEST
I WANTED u more THAN I WANTED ME
I rememBer my last Thought at night was of u
and my FIRST Thought iN the morning was of u
It has BEEN a long time since I've actually
sat and adored u but every once in awhile
your beautiful smile guides me through a day
I hear u R with another and u R expecting
I wish u good Luck He is lucky 2 be able
2 wake up 2 u each morning
C u iN Heaven!

Tupac Amaru Shak

Carmencita of the Bronx!

Dedicated 2 Carmen

u saw innocence at its best

I wanted u more than I wanted me

I remember my last thought at night was of u

and my first thought in the morning was of u

It has been a long time since I've actually

sat and adored u but every once in awhile

your beautiful smile guides me through a day

I hear u R with another and u R expecting

I wish u good luck he is lucky 2 be able

2 wake up 2 u each morning

c u in heaven!

EVERY WORD
            CUTS 2 THE HEART

CONVERSATIONS R ENDED
            BE 4 THEY START

is This what u WANT ?

        is This what I want?

            is this what
                    MUST BE ?

This is NOT A GAME

            This is A LOVE
        one should be played
        The other cherished

I feel 2 HEARTS BREAKING ...

    is This what u WANT
    is This what I want
    is This what MUST BE 0

Untitled

Every word
      cuts 2 the heart
conversations R ended
      be4 they start
is this what u want?
      is this what I want?
         is this what
            must be?

This is not a game
      This is a love
      one should be played
      The other cherished
I feel 2 hearts breaking. . .

      is this what u want?
      is this what I want?
      is this what must be?

you ask me 2 communicate
What it is I feel within
I Search 4 words 2 assist
But I find none 2 help me Begin
I guess love is just complicated
                    Love
                         is
                            Just
                               complicated.

I Thought I Knew my Heart's Desire
I thought I quenched my Burning Fire
I thought I wanted "A"
But "A" was 2 mixed up with "B"
Then "C" made me more confused
So "A" turned off me and "B" feels
better. "C" is upset and lonely
and me, I think love is complicated
                 Love
                      is
                         Just
                            complicated.

                    2-Pac

Love Is Just Complicated

you ask me 2 communicate
what it is I feel within
I search 4 words 2 assist
but I find none 2 help me begin
I guess love is just complicated

                Love

                        is

                                just

                                          complicated.

I thought I knew my heart's desire
I thought I quenched my burning fire
I thought I wanted "A"
But "A" was 2 mixed up with "B"
Then "C" made me more confused
So "A" turned off me and "B" feels
better. "C" is upset and lonely
and me, I think Love is complicated.

                Love

                        is

                                just

                                          complicated.

ELIZABETH

A different Love   From B.S.A.

I Remember when u were Lost
and your soul was in the wind
IT was at this awkward moment
 that u and I Became friends
But Then your soul was found
and u discovered ~~the~~ celibacy
But with this u forgot about me
and our Bond was a memory
 And Now I C u felt it
the Bond we made Before
 I pray 2 God it stands
and severes never more

Elizabeth
A Different Love

From B.S.A.

I remember when u were LOST
and your soul was in the wind
It was at this awkward moment
that u and I became friends
But then your soul was found
and u discovered celibacy
But with this u forgot about me
and our bond was a memory
And now I c u felt it
the bond we made before
I pray 2 God it stands
and severs never more

KNOW my ♥ HAS LIED BEFORE

I know my heart has lied before
but now it speaks with honesty
of an invisible bond of friendship
that was formed in secrecy
Coming from me this may seem hard
but 2 GOD I swear its' truth
We R friends for eternity
and Forever I will always love u.

With All My Heart,
&
"j"
"Spirit"

P.S. JUST SO U DON'T FORGET THAT
I AM HERE FOR U. U R A TRUE
FRIEND

I Know My Heart Has Lied Before

I know my heart has lied before
but now it speaks with honesty
of an invisible bond of friendship
that was formed in secrecy
Coming from me this may seem hard
but 2 GOD I swear it's truth
We R friends for eternity
and Forever I will always love u

With All My Heart,
&
"Spirit"

P.S. Just so u don't forget that
    I am here for u. U R a true
    friend.

FROM FIRST GLANCE,
4 Michelle From Z AP's
FEB 1, 1990

From First Glance I KNOW exactly what would Be
u and I Have perfect Hearts Destined one Day 2 Be
The circumstances Don't even matter Because my Heart lies
Never
And if u don't admit 2 this it is u who will Be Surpri

From First Glance

4 Michelle From Zap's

Feb 1, 1990

From first glance I know exactly what would Be

u and I have perfect hearts destined one day 2 Be

The circumstances don't even matter because my heart
  never lies

And if u don't admit 2 this it is u who will be surprised

1 FOR April

2 Me your Name Alone is poetry
I barely KNOW u AND Already
I can't explain This feeling I feel
             4 APRIL
I WANT 2 C u From THE MOMENT
u Leave my side Til the MOMENT u return
My NONchalant cold heart Finally has eyes only
             4 April
So NOW I risk it all
Just 4 The feeling of joy u Bring me
I accept the ridicule
in exchange for the words u share with me
All OF THIS & MUCH MORE I WILL DO
             4 APRIL

1 for April

2 me your name alone is poetry

I barely know u and already

I can't explain this feeling I feel

        4 APRIL

I want 2 c u from the moment

u leave my side till the moment u return

My nonchalant cold heart finally has eyes only

        4 APRIL

So now I risk it all

Just 4 the feeling of joy u bring me

I accept the ridicule

in exchange for the words u share with me

All of this & much more I will do

        4 APRIL

Wife 4 Life

Dedicated 2 April

I Hope u heard me when I asked
u that night 2 be my wife
Not for this year or Next
But mine for all your life
2 Accept me when I sin
and understand me when I fail
Not 2 mention standing the rain
which comes down as hard as hail
I am not the Best of men
My faults could scare the night
But my Heart is always pure 2 my wife 4 life

Wife 4 Life

Dedicated 2 April

I hope u heard me when I asked
u that night 2 be my wife
Not for this year or next
But mine for all your life
2 accept me when I sin
and understand me when I fail
Not 2 mention standing the rain
which comes down as hard as hail
I am not the best of men
My faults could scare the night
But my heart is always pure 2 my wife 4 life

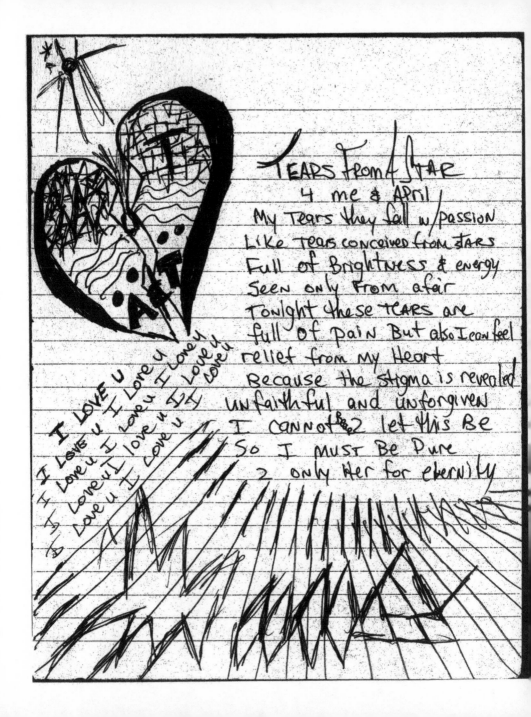

Tears From 4 Star
4 me & April
My Tears they fall w/ passion
Like tears conceived from stars
Full of Brightness & energy
Seen only From afair
Tonight these Tears are
full of pain But also I can feel
relief from my Heart
Because the stigma is revealed
unfaithful and unforgiven
I cannot 2 let this Be
So I MUST Be Pure
2 only Her for eternity

I LOVE U I love u I love u I love u love u
I Love u I love u I I love u
I Love u I love u
I Love u I love u

Tears from a Star

4 Me & April

My tears they fall with passion
Like tears conceived from stars
Full of brightness & energy
Seen only from afar
Tonight these tears are
full of pain but also I can feel
relief from my heart
Because the stigma is revealed
unfaithful and unforgiven
I cannot bear 2 let this be
So I must be pure
2 only her for eternity

MARCH 1st = THE Day AFTER April

Dedicated 2 the Divorce of Me & April

Today I wake & feel even lonelier
But I c positive potential
My Heart shook much like the Quake
then the pain was gone
the arctic breeze formed the fortress
Barricading my fragile Heart from Pain

It ~~Ain't true~~ is Nor That I Don't Love U
and it was because I Did love U
that I must move on
As Long as I Breathe
I will remember

" WE AS 2 "

March 1st—The Day After April
Dedicated 2 the Divorce of Me & April

Today I wake and feel even lonelier
But I c positive potential
My heart shook much like the quake
Then the pain was gone
The arctic breeze formed the fortress
Barricading my fragile heart from Pain

It is not that I don't love u
and it was because I did love u
that I must move on
as long as I breathe
I will remember
   "WE AS 2"

WHY MUST U BE UNFAITHFUL?
4 WOMEN

MEN!

U SHOULDN'T LISTEN 2 your selfish ♥
IT doesn't really HAVE A BRAIN
Besides keeping u ALIVE
ITS existence is IN VAIN
How could I be so mean,
and say your heart has no place"?
Because MORTAL MEN FALL IN LOVE AGAIN
as Fast as they change their face
I may be cruel, BUT THINK awhile about
the hearts That u have Broken
Match That with the empty vows
and broken promises u've spoken
I AM NOT Saying females R perfect
Because MEN we know it's not True
But why must u be unfaithful
If her heart is True 2 u !!!!

Shakur

Why Must U Be Unfaithful

4 Women

MEN!
u shouldn't listen 2 your selfish heart
It doesn't really have a brain
Besides keeping u alive
Its existence is in vain
"How could I be so mean,
and say your heart has no place?"
Because mortal men fall in love again
as fast as they change their face
I may be cruel, but think awhile about
The hearts that u have broken
Match that with the empty vows
and broken promises u've spoken
I am not saying females R perfect
Because men we know it's not true
But why must u be unfaithful
If her heart is true 2 u!!!!

The power of a smile
                    4 Renee'

The power of a gun can kill
and the power of Fire can Burn
The power of wind can chill
and the power of the mind can learn
The power of anger can rage
inside until it tears u apart
But the Power of a smile
especially yours can heal a frozen Heart ♡

The Power of a Smile

4 Reneé

The power of a gun can kill
and the power of Fire can Burn
The power of wind can chill
and the power of the mind can learn
The power of anger can rage
inside until it tears u apart
But the Power of a Smile
especially yours can heal a frozen Heart

Genesis (The Rebirth of my Heart)
Dedicated 2 Renee Ross

First There was nothing
Not even the faint echo of a Song
Loneliness was Daily 4 me
until u came along
There was a gleam of Stars in your eyes
I Thought I'd Never feel this way again
But u were the one 2 reach into my Heart
And find in me a Friend
I could Not ignore the magnetism
That I felt when u were Near
And Any Problems Plaguing my mind
would Suddenly Disappear
was the Rebirth of my Heart
The Day u Became my Friend
Because I Knew From the Moment
I Held u that I would Find love again

Genesis (The Rebirth of My Heart)

Dedicated 2 Renee Ross

First there was nothing
Not even the faint echo of a song
Loneliness was daily 4 me
   until u came along
There was a gleam of stars in your eyes
I thought I'd never feel this way again
But u were the one 2 reach into my heart
And find in me a Friend
I could not ignore the magnetism
that I felt when u were near
And any problems plaguing my mind
would suddenly disappear
It was the rebirth of my heart
The day u became my friend
Because I knew from the moment
I held u that I would find love again

LOVE WITHIN A STORM
4 Elizabeth

We made Love within a storm
in the midst of passion and chaos
Somewhere, somehow our true bond
of friendship was lost

In the eye of the storm
the rain always falls harder
those who prevail this Trauma
will ~~live~~ learn 2 Bring their love farther

But now the storm Has passed
and the seas of our friendship R calm
But as long as I live I will rememember
the Love within the storm

Love Within a Storm

4 Elizabeth

We made love within a storm
in the midst of passion and chaos
somewhere, somehow our true bond
of friendship was lost

In the eye of the storm
The rain always falls harder
Those who prevail this trauma
will learn 2 bring their love farther

But now the storm has passed
and the seas of our friendship R calm
But as long as I live I will remember
the love within the storm

WHAT CAN I OFFER HER ?

ALL OF MY LIFE I DREAMED of MEETING ONE
WITH immense BEAUTY, and ONCE I found her
I would charm her and SHE'D BE MINE
forever.

I Have found her and indeed she is all
I WISHED for and more but she is
NOT charmed Nor intriqued, Then I
Think 2 myself "What Can I offer her?"
The tears warm my eyes and blur my
VISION I stick 2 my stance of BRAVADO
and give her the Same uNiNterested look
She gave me. She was so beautiful
BUT what can I offer her

What Can I Offer Her?

All of my life I dreamed of meeting one
with immense beauty, and once I found her
I would charm her and she'd be mine
forever.

I have found her and indeed she is all
I wished for and more but she is
not charmed nor intrigued. Then I
think 2 myself "What can I offer her?"
The tears warm my eyes and blur my
vision. I stick 2 my stance of bravado
and give her the same uninterested look
she gave me. She was so beautiful
But what can I offer her.

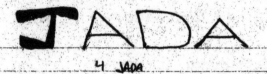

JADA

4 JADA

U R The omega of my Heart
The foundation 4 my conception of Love
when I think of what a Black woman should be
it's u that I First Think of

u will never fully understand
How Deeply my Heart Feels 4 u
I worry that we'll grow apart
and I'll end up losing u

U Bring me 2 climax without sex
and u do it all with regal grace
u R my Heart in Human Form
a Friend I could never replace

Jada

4 Jada

u R the omega of my Heart
The foundation 4 my conception of Love
when I think of what a Black woman should be
it's u that I First think of

u will never fully understand
How Deeply my Heart Feels 4 u
I worry that we'll grow apart
and I'll end up losing u

u bring me 2 climax without sex
and u do it all with regal grace
u R my Heart in Human Form
a Friend I could never replace

The Tears in Cupid's Eyes
4 JADA

the Day u chose 2 leave me
it rained constantly outside
In Truth I Swore the rain 2 be
The Tears in Cupid's eyes

The Tears in Cupid's Eyes

4 Jada

The day u chose 2 leave me
it rained constantly outside
In truth I swore the rain 2 be
The tears in Cupid's eyes

CUPID'S SMILE II

I ran outside 2 feel the rain
and I stayed outside awhile
when the rain was done along came the sun
and this was Cupid's Smile !

Cupid's Smile II

I ran outside 2 feel the rain
and I stayed outside awhile
when the rain was done along came the sun
and this was Cupid's Smile!

WHAT 👁 SEE ?

WITH my eyes closed I can c
we Have a chance 2 Discover ecstacy
But The clouds of DouBT HAVE made u Blind
So u R afraid of the emotions that u may find
I KNOW THAT u've Been HurT Before
But This is No excuse 4 u 2 ignore
The seed THAT cupid planted, in Hopes THAT we would sow
THis infant emotion Deserves 2 BreaTHe So why won't u let it grow
A Neglected flower will wiTHer and on its own it will surely Die
But with honesty, Passion, and Mutual respect we can Soar Beyond the Sky
So please don't follow what u c follow the ryTHym within your heart
Believe in me Though u cannot c what lies within the Dark

What I See!

With my eyes closed I can c
we have a chance 2 discover ecstasy
but the clouds of doubt have made u blind
so u R afraid of the emotions that u may find
I know that u've been hurt before
but this is no excuse 4 u 2 ignore
the seed that cupid planted, in hopes that we would sow
This infant emotion deserves 2 breathe so why won't u
   let it grow
A neglected flower will wither and on its own it will
   surely die
But with honesty, passion, and mutual respect we can
   soar beyond the sky
So please don't follow what u c follow the rhythm within
   your heart
Believe in me though u cannot c what lies within the
   Dark

In The Midst of Passion (ADULTERY)

In The midst of passion 2 figures stand
emerged in eestasy joined hand & hand
words R unnecessary feelings R Heard
The body takes control Deaf 2 words
It is at this stage that I think of u
In gratitude 4 this joy, u have exposed me 2
Each Day is Bright with you as the Dawn
with the collapse of each night a strong bond is born
In the midst of passion I Remember your kiss
I Reminisse about your touch and suddenly miss
The scent u wear and the tone of your voice
Only u can be my choice
In the midst of passion
        I C U & me
    Lost in constant eestasy..//

In the Midst of Passion

(Adultery)

In the midst of passion 2 figures stand
emerged in ecstasy joined hand and hand
words R unnecessary feelings R heard
the body takes control deaf 2 words
It is at this stage that I think of u
in gratitude 4 this joy u have exposed me 2
Each Day is Bright with you as the Dawn
with the collapse of each night a strong bond is born
In the midst of passion I remember your kiss
I reminisce about your touch and suddenly miss
the scent u wear and the tone of your voice
Only u can be my choice
In the midst of passion
I c u & me
Lost in constant ecstasy!!

2 PEOPLE WITH 1 WISH

There were 2 people with one wish
2 Live a Life filled with Love
2 GOD They would pray That 2gether They'd stay
under the stars above
But someone else MADE A WISH
AT THE SAME Time on THe same BreaTH
And although the WISH 4 love was granted
So was this evil WISH 4 DeaTH
NOW I MAKE A wish
Sealed WITH TEARS AND LAUGHTER
IT is My Nish THAT THese 2 Loves
R Reunited in THe HereaFTer

2 People with 1 Wish

There were 2 people with one wish
2 live a Life filled with Love
2 GOD they would pray that 2gether they'd stay
under the stars above
But someone else made a wish
at the same time on the same breath
And although the wish 4 love was granted
so was this evil wish 4 Death
Now I make a wish
sealed with tears and laughter
It is my wish that these 2 loves
R reunited in the hereafter

Hours Pass By

I THINK OF u IN my Arms
And what it would be like 2 Make Lov.
I think of u raising my SEED
And WHAT THEY'D BE MADE OF
I THINK OF How Alone I was.
Before u came 2 Be
I Think of the Joy I felt
when u said u THOUGHT of me
Hours Pass By and cupid cries
until we meet again
I'm proud 2 Be the Heart u
Choose 2 make a Friend

Hours Pass By

I think of u in my arms
   and what it would be like 2 make love
I think of u raising my SEED
   and what they'd be made of
I think of how alone I was
   before u came 2 be
I think of the joy I felt
   when u said u thought of me
I'm proud 2 be the heart u
   choose 2 make a friend
Hours pass by and cupid cries
   until we meet again

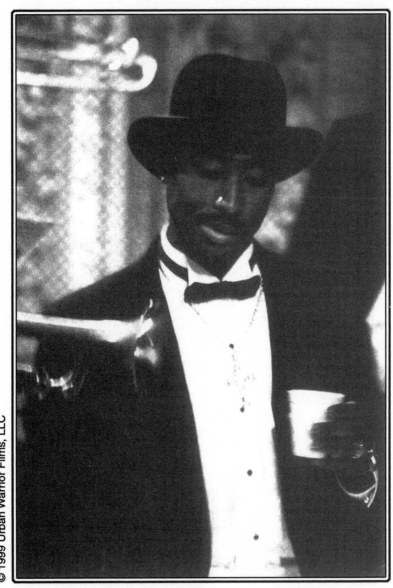

Just A Breath
of Freedom

JUST A BREATH OF FREEDOM
4 Nelson Mandela

Held captive 4 your politics
They wanted 2 break your soul
they ordered the extermination
of all minds they couldn't control
4 u the fate was far worse
Than just a brutal homicide
They caged u like an animal
and watched u slowly die inside
As u breath your first air of freedom
on the day u become a free men
Raise your regal brow in pride
4 now you R in God's Hands
The life of many were given
So that this day would one day come
That the devils in power at Pretoria
Would pay for the evil crimes they've done

Just a Breath of Freedom

4 Nelson Mandela

Held captive 4 your politics
They wanted 2 break your soul
They ordered the extermination
of all minds they couldn't control
4 u the fate was far worse
than just a brutal homicide
They caged u like an animal
and watched u slowly die inside
As u Breathe your first air of freedom
on the day u become a free man
Raise your Regal Brow in Pride
4 now you R in God's Hands
The life of many were given
so that the day would one day come
That the devils in Power at Pretoria
would pay for the evil crimes they've done

FOR MRS HAWKINS
                    IN Memory of Yusef Hawkins

THis poem is Adressed 2 Mrs Hawkins
WHo lost her son 2 a racist Society
I'm Not out 2 offend the positive souls
ONLY The racist Dogs WHo Lied 2 me
AN American culture plague with Nights
Like the Night Yusef was Killed
if it were reversed it would be the work
of a Savage but this white killer was just STRONG willed
But Mrs Hawkins As Sure As I'm a Panther
with the Blood of Malcolm in my viens
America will Never rest
  if Yusef Dies iN VAiN!

For Mrs. Hawkins

In Memory of Yusef Hawkins

This poem is addressed 2 Mrs. Hawkins
who lost her son 2 a racist society
I'm not out 2 offend the positive souls
only the racist dogs who lied 2 me
An American culture plagued with nights
like the night Yusef was killed
if it were reversed it would be the work
of a savage but this white killer was just strong-willed
But Mrs. Hawkins as sure as I'm a Panther
with the blood of Malcolm in my veins
America will never rest
if Yusef dies in vain!

THE SUN AND THE MOON

Your ways R similar 2 the rays of the sun
warm 2 many but 2 strong 4 some
The more u R needed the brighter u shine
watched 4 2 long and your brilliance will blind
The s of mortal men who threaten u with doom
They regret 2 c u set but it is time 4 the moon

The Sun and the Moon

Your ways R similar 2 the rays of the sun
Warm 2 many but 2 strong 4 some
The more u R needed the brighter u shine
Watched 4 2 long and your brilliance will blind
The eyes of mortal men who threaten u with doom
They regret 2 c u set but it is time 4 the moon

"FALLEN STAR"

4 Huey P. Newton

They could never understand
~~what~~ u set out 2 do
instead they chose 2
ridicule u
when u got weak
They loved the sight
of your dimming
and flickering starlight
How could they understand what was so intricate
2 Be loved by so many, so intimate
they wanted 2 c your lifeless corpse
This way u could not alter the course
of ignorance that they have set
2 make my people forget
what they have done for much 2 long
2 just forget and carry on
I had ~~2~~ loved u forever Because of who u R
~~wonder and cared~~
And now I mourn our fallen star

"Fallen Star"

4 Huey P. Newton

They could never understand
what u set out 2 do
instead they chose 2
ridicule u
when u got weak
They loved the sight
of your dimming
and flickering starlight
How could they understand what was so intricate
2 be loved by so many, so intimate
they wanted 2 c your lifeless corpse
This way u could not alter the course
of ignorance that they have set
2 make my people forget
what they have done for much 2 long
2 just forget and carry on
I had loved u forever because of who u R
And now I mourn our fallen star

GOVERNMENT ASSISTANCE
or
MY SOUL

It would be like a panther
asking a panther hunter
4 some meat. All
High School Dropouts R NOT DUMB
All unemployed aren't lazy
and there R many Days I hunger
But I would go hungry and homeless
Before the American Government gets my Soul

Government Assistance
or
My Soul

It would be like a panther
asking a panther hunter
4 some meat, all
High school dropouts R not DUMB
All unemployed aren't lazy
and there R many days I hunger
But I would go hungry and homeless
Before the American Government gets my soul

FAMILY TREE

4 MOTHER

Because we all spring
From Different Trees
Does not mean
We are NOT CREATED Equally

Is the True Beauty in the Tree
or in the vast forest in which it breaths
THE Tree must Fight 2 Breed
Among the Evils of the weeds

I FIND greatness in the Tree
That grows against all odds
it Blossoms in Darkness
and gives Birth 2 promising Pods.

I was The Tree who grew from weeds
and wasn't meant 2 Be
Ashamed I am NOT in fact I am proud
of my Thriving Family Tree

Family Tree

4 Mother

Because we all spring
from different trees
does not mean
we are not created equally

Is the true beauty in the tree
or in the vast forest in which it breathes
the tree must fight 2 breed
among the evils of the weeds

I find greatness in the tree
that grows against all odds
it blossoms in darkness
and gives birth 2 promising pods.

I was the tree who grew from weeds
and wasn't meant 2 be
ashamed I'm not in fact I am proud
of my thriving family tree

OR MY SOUL   Dedicated 2 Moms

Dedicated 2 THE Powers
THAT B

The choice is No Stranger 2 poverty
your Soul or Government Assistance
I'm 18 in a Country with No paTH
4 A young unaddicted Black youth with a Dream
INSTEAD I am giving the Ultimatum:

Or My Soul

Dedicated 2 Moms
Dedicated 2 the Powers That B

The choice is no stranger 2 poverty
your soul or Government Assistance
I'm 18 in a country with no path
4 a young unaddicted Black youth with a Dream
Instead I am giving the Ultimatum.

WHEN URE HERO FALLS
4 my Hero (my Mother)

when your hero falls from grace
all fairy tales R uncovered
Myths exposed and pain Magnified
The greatest pain Discovered
U Taught me 2 Be strong
But I'm confused 2 c u So weak
u said Never 2 give up
and it hurts 2 c u welcome defeat
When ure Hero falls so Do the stars
and So does the perception of tomorrow
without my Hero there is only
me alone 2 deal with my Sorrow.
your Heart ceases 2 work
and your soul is not happy at all
what R u expected 2 Do
when ure only Hero falls

When Ure Hero Falls

4 My Hero (My Mother)

when your hero falls from grace
all fairy tales R uncovered
myths exposed and pain magnified
the greatest pain discovered
u taught me 2 be strong
but I'm confused 2 c u so weak
u said never 2 give up
and it hurts 2 c u welcome defeat
when ure Hero falls so do the stars
and so does the perception of tomorrow
without my Hero there is only
me alone 2 deal with my sorrow.
your Heart ceases 2 work
and your soul is not happy at all
what R u expected 2 do
when ure only Hero falls

UNTITLED

Strength is overcome by weakness
Joy is overcome by Pain
The night is overcome by Brightness
and Love — it remains the same

E

Untitled

Strength is overcome by weakness
Joy is overcome by Pain
The night is overcome by Brightness
and Love—it remains the same

"U R Ripping Us Apart !!!"

Dedicated 2 Crack

Before u came the Triangle never broke
we were bonded and melded as one
But as the 2 pushed u away
The one got weak and embraced u
and now u r ripping us apart

The worst feeling of helplessness
The greatest pain has rested in my heart
The vision of heaven fades
and the nightmare of loneliness has started

My Hero has been defeated by you
and now what can I do
Watch as u Destroy us
and our love is finally Through

I know the worst is Here
I feel it in my Heart
u got into the circle
Now you're tearing us apart !!!!!!!!!!!!!

!

"U R Ripping Us Apart !!!"

Dedicated 2 Crack

Before u came the triangle never broke
we were bonded and melded as one
But as the 2 pushed u away
The one got weak and embraced u
and now u R ripping us apart

The worst feeling of helplessness
The greatest pain has rested in my heart
The vision of heaven fades
and the nightmare of loneliness has started

My Hero has been defeated by you
and now what can I do
watch as u destroy us
and our love is finally through

I know the worst is here
I feel it in my Heart
u got into the circle
now you're tearing us apart !!!!!!!!!!!!!

A River that Flows Forever
4 mother

As Long as some suffer
The River Flows Forever
As Long As there is pain
The River Flows Forever
As strong as a smile can be
the River will Flow Forever
And as long as u R with me
we'll ride the River together

T

A River That Flows Forever

4 Mother

As long as some suffer
  The River Flows Forever
As long as there is pain
  The River Flows Forever
As strong as a smile can be
  The River will Flow Forever
And as long as u R with me
  we'll ride the River Together

Can U C The Pride In The Panther

Can u c the pride in the pantha
as He glows in splendor and grace
Toppling obstacles placed in the way
of the progression of his Race

Can u c the pride in the Pantha
as she nurtures her young all alone
The seed must grow regardless
of the fact that its planted in stone

CAN'T u c the Pride in the panthas
as they unify as one
The flower blooms with brilliance
and outshines the rays of the sun

Can U C the Pride in the Panther

Can u c the pride in the pantha
as he glows in splendor and grace
Toppling OBSTACLES placed in the way
of the progression of his race

Can u c the pride in the Pantha
as she nurtures her young all alone
The seed must grow regardless
of the fact that it's planted in stone

Can't u c the pride in the panthas
as they unify as one
The flower blooms with brilliance
and outshines the rays of the sun

Tears of a Teenage Mother

He's Bragging about his New Jordans
   The Baby Just ran out of Milk
He's Buying gold every 2 weeks
   the Baby Just ran out of Pampers
He's buying cloths for his New girl
   & the Baby Just ran out of Medicine
u ask for Money for the Baby
   The Daddy Just ran out the Door

Tears of a Teenage Mother

He's bragging about his new Jordans
  the Baby just ran out of milk
He's buying gold every 2 weeks
  the Baby just ran out of Pampers
He's buying clothes for his new girl
  & the Baby just ran out of medicine
u ask for money for the Baby
  the Daddy just ran out the Door

" WHERE THERE IS A WILL ...."

where There is a will
There is A way
2 Search and discover
a Better Day

where a positive heart
is all u NEED
2 Rise BeyonD
and Succeed

where young minds grow
and respect each other
Based on their Deeds
and Not their color

when Times R DIM
say as I say..
"where There is A will
there is a way!"

"Where There Is a Will. . . ."

Where there is a will
there is a way
2 search and discover
a better day

Where a positive heart
is all u need
2 Rise Beyond
and succeed

Where young minds grow
and respect each other
based on their Deeds
and not their color

When times R dim
say as I say
"Where there is a will
There is a way!"

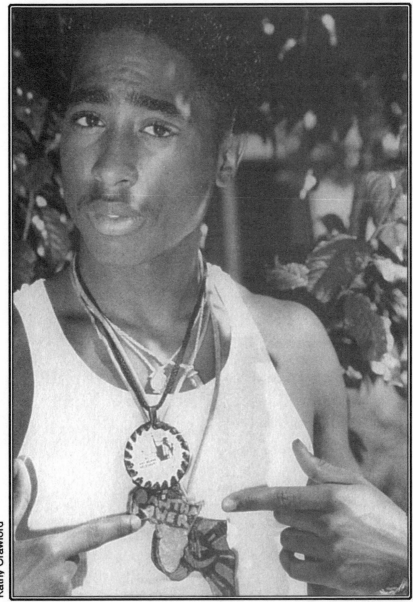

Liberty Needs Glasses

Liberty Needs Glasses

excuse me But lady liBeRTy NeeDs glasses
AND So Does mrs Justice By her siDe
BoTh 9he BroaDs R BliND AS BaTs
Stumbling THru the System
Justice Bumbed iNTo MuTuIu aND
Trippin' oN GeroNimo PraTT
But STeppeD right over OliveR
AND his crookeD partNer RoNNie
Justice STubbeD her Big Toe oN MaNDela
AND liBerTy was misquoTeD By the iNDiaNS
sIavery was a learNiNG DHAse
ForgoTTeN with out a verDicT
while Justice is oN a rampage
4 eNDaNgereD SurviviNg Black males
I mean Really if anyone Really valueD life
aND careD about the masses
They'D Take em BoTh 2 PeN opTical
aND geT 2 paire of Glasses

Liberty Needs Glasses

excuse me but Lady Liberty needs glasses
And so does Mrs. Justice by her side
Both the broads R blind as bats
Stumbling thru the system
Justice bumped into Mutulu and
Trippin' on Geronimo Pratt
But stepped right over Oliver
And his crooked partner Ronnie
Justice stubbed her Big Toe on Mandela
And liberty was misquoted by the Indians
slavery was a learning phase
Forgotten without a verdict
while Justice is on a rampage
4 endangered surviving Black males
I mean really if anyone really valued life
and cared about the masses
They'd take 'em both 2 Pen Optical
and get 2 pairs of glasses

How Can We Be Free

Sometimes I wonder about this ~~grace~~ race
Because we must be blind as hell
2 think we live in equality
While Nelson Mandela rots in a jail cell
Where ~~the~~ the shores of Howard Beach
are full of Afrikan Corpses
And those ~~that~~ do live 2 be 18
Bumrush 2 join the Armed Forces
This so called "Home of the Brave"
Why isn't anybody Backing us up!
When they © these crooked ass Redneck cops
constantly Jacking us up
Now I Bet some punk will say I'm Racist
I can tell by the way you smile at me
Then I remember George Jackson, Huey Newton
and Geronimo ~~and~~ 2 hell with Lady Liberty

How Can We Be Free

Sometimes I wonder about this race
Because we must be blind as hell
2 think we live in equality
while Nelson Mandela rots in a jail cell
Where the shores of Howard Beach
are full of Afrikan corpses
And those that do live 2 be 18
Bumrush 2 join the Armed Forces
This so called "Home of the Brave"
why isn't anybody Backing us up!
When they c these crooked ass Redneck cops
constantly Jacking us up
Now I bet some punk will say I'm racist
I can tell by the way you smile at me
then I remember George Jackson, Huey Newton
and Geronimo 2 hell with Lady Liberty

THE 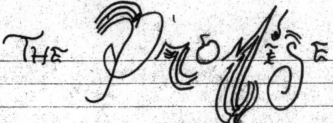 Promise

"I will give u Liberty, But First give me ure spirit,
This I must confiscate Because the evil Fear it"
I Too would be Afraid of passion governed By reason
An open miND 2 trying Times when corruption is in season
The promise that they claim
   2 Be completely True
is hypocrisy at it's finest
  A Trick 2 silence u
Never will I Believe a promise
from the masters of the Art
Trickery Does Not Succeed
With Those With Honest Hearts

The Promise

"I will give u liberty, but first give me ure spirit,
This I must confiscate because the evil fear it."
I too would be afraid of passion governed by reason
An open mind 2 trying times when corruption is in
    season
The promise that they claim
    2 be completely true
is hypocrisy at its finest
A trick 2 silence u
never will I believe a promise
from the masters of the Art
Trickery does not succeed
with those with Honest Hearts

AND 2morrow

TODAY is FILLED WITH ANGER
FUELED WITH HIDDEN HATE
Scared OF BEING outcast
Afraid of common FATE
TODAY is BUILT ON TRAGEDIES
WHICH NO ONE WANTS 2 Face
NIGHTmares 2 Humanities
and Morally Disgraced
TONIGHT is filled with rage
Violence IN the Air
cHildren BreD with Ruthlessness
Because NO ONE AT Home cares
Tonight I Lay my HeaD DOWN
But the pressure NeVeR stops
GROWING aT my SANITY
CONTENT when I Am Dropped
But 2morrow I c change
A chance 2 Build A New
BuilT ON spirit, intent of HeArT
and ideals BaseD ON truth
AND Tomorrow I wake with SecOND WiND
AND STRONG Because of PriDe
2 KNOW I FOUGHT WITH ALL my Heart 2 Keep my
                                        DReAM ALive

And 2morrow

Today is filled with anger
Fueled with hidden hate
Scared of being outcast
Afraid of common fate
Today is built on tragedies
which no one wants 2 face
Nightmares 2 humanities
and morally disgraced
Tonight is filled with rage
Violence in the air
Children bred with ruthlessness
Because no one at home cares
Tonight I lay my head down
But the pressure never stops
gnawing at my sanity
content when I am dropped
But 2morrow I c change
A chance 2 build anew
Built on spirit, intent of heart
and ideals based on truth
And 2morrow I wake with second wind
And strong because of pride
2 know I fought with all my heart 2 keep my dream alive

NO-WIN

(DReam poem)

Backed into a corner
alone and very confused
Tired of running away
My ~~Manhood~~ has been abused
Not my choice 2 Be so blunt
But u must fight fire with flame
I allowed myself 2 run once
and was haunted by the shame
if I must kill I will and if I must Do it
I would but the Situation is a NO WIN

No-Win

(Dream poem)

Backed into a corner
alone and very confused
Tired of running away
My manhood has been abused
Not my choice 2 be so blunt
But u must fight fire with flame
I allowed myself 2 run once
and was haunted by the shame
if I must kill I will and if I must do it again
I would but the situation is a no-win

The unanswerable ?
Question:
WHEN WILL THERE BE PEACE ON
EARTH?
Answer: WHEN THE EARTH FALLS
2 Pieces!!

The Unanswerable?

QUESTION:

WHEN WILL THERE BE PEACE ON EARTH?

ANSWER: WHEN THE EARTH FALLS 2 PIECES!!

NIGHTMARES

Dedicated 2 those curious

I pour my Heart in2 this poem
and Look 4 the meaning of Life
the rich and powerful always prevail
and the less fortunate strive through strife
MISTAKES R MADE 2 Be 4 given
We R 2 young 2 stress and suffer
The path of purity and positivety
has always ridden rougher
Your ~~INSATIABLE~~ Desire 2 find perfection
Has made your faults magnify
curiousity can take Blame
For the evil that makes u cry
It isn't a good feeling when u disobey your Heart
the nightmares haunt your Soul and your nerves Rip apart

Nightmares

Dedicated 2 Those Curious

I pour my heart in2 this poem
and look 4 the meaning of Life
the rich and powerful always prevail
and the less fortunate strive through strife
MISTAKES R MADE 2 be 4given
we R 2 young 2 stress and suffer
The path of purity and positivity
has always ridden rougher
Your insatiable desire 2 find perfection
Has made your faults magnify
curiosity can take Blame
For the evil that makes u cry
It isn't a good feeling when u disobey your Heart
The nightmares haunt your Soul and your nerves R
   ripped apart

SO say GOODBYE

NOV 20

I'M GOING IN2 THIS NOT KNOWING WHAT I'LL FIND
BUT I'VE DECIDED 2 FOLLOW MY HEART & ABANDON MY MIND
AND IF THERE BE PAIN I KNOW THAT AT LEAST I GAVE MY ALL
AND IT IS BETTER 2 HAVE LOVED & LOST THAN 2 NOT LOVE AT ALL
IN THE MORNING I MAY WAKE 2 SMILE OR MAYBE 2 CRY
BUT FIRST 2 THOSE OF MY PAST I MUST SAY GOODBYE

So I Say GOODBYE

Nov 20

I'm going in2 this not knowing what I'll find
but I've decided 2 follow my heart and abandon my mind
and if there be pain I know that at least I gave my all
and it is better 2 have loved and lost than 2 not love at all
In the morning I may wake 2 smile or maybe 2 cry
but first 2 those of my past I must say goodbye

In The Event Of My Demise

Dedicated 2 those curious

In the event of my Demise
when my heart can beat no more
I Hope I Die For A Principle
or A Belief that I had lived 4
I will die Before my Time
Because I feel the shadow's Depth
so much I wanted 2 accomplish
Before I reached my Death
I have come 2 grips with the possibility
and wiped the last tear from my eyes
I Loved All who were Positive
In the event of my Demise!

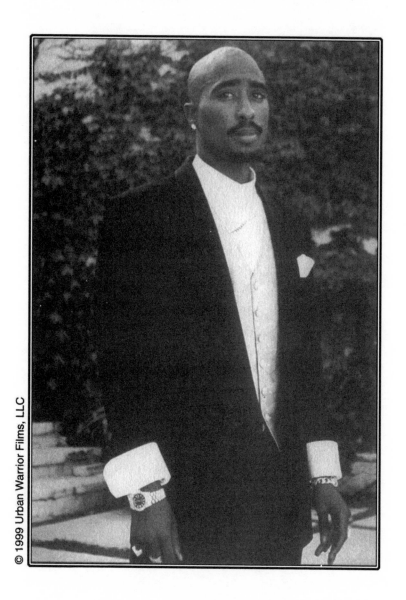

TUPAC AMARU SHAKUR
1971–1996

2Pac Fan Club

To join the 2PAC legacy fan club send $25 (U.S.) or $30 (non-U.S.) check or money order (no cash) along with your application to:

Membership 2PAC Fan Club

5231 East Memorial Drive

PMB 222

Stone Mountain, GA 30083

Visit our website at www.2PAClegacy.com

Call the information hotline at (404) 508-0901

--------------------cut here----------------------------cut here------------------------

First Name: _____ Last Name: _____

Address: _____

City: _____ State: _____ Zip Code: _____

e-mail: _____

t-shirt size: S   M   L   XL   XXL

Your one-year membership includes a quarterly newsletter, 2PAC t-shirt, and a photograph.